No. CLI

THE MINOR DRAMA

THE

DUTCHMAN'S GHOST;

OR,

ALL RIGHT.

An Original Farce, in One Act.

BY S. BARRY

WITH CAST OF CHARACTERS, STAGE BUSINESS, COSTUMES, RELATIVE POSITIONS, &c., &c.

AS PERFORMED AT THE PRINCIPAL AMERICAN THEATRES

NEW YORK:
SAMUEL FRENCH & SON,
PUBLISHERS,
38 EAST 14TH ST., UNION SQ.

LONDON:
SAMUEL FRENCH,
PUBLISHER,
89 STRAND.

THE MINOR DRAMA.

The Acting Edition.

No. CLI.

THE DUTCHMAN'S GHOST;

OR,

ALL RIGHT.

An Original Farce, in One Act.

BY S. BARRY,

Author of "A Romance in High Life," "Coachman and the Heiress," "Persecuted Dutchman," "Capital Prize," "Dick Tarleton," "Spirit of '76," "Who is the Father?" "A Leaf of Crime," "It runs in the Family," &c., &c.

TO WHICH ARE ADDED

A Description of the Costume—Cast of the Characters—Entrances and Exits—Relative Positions of the Performers on the Stage, and the whole of the Stage Business.

New York:	London:
SAMUEL FRENCH & SON,	SAMUEL FRENCH,
PUBLISHERS,	PUBLISHER,
38 EAST 14TH STREET.	89, STRAND.

Cast of the Characters.—[THE DUTCHMAN'S GHOST.]

	Original, Bowery, 1857.	*National,* 1858.
HANS BARTH	Mr. S. Barry.	Mr. S. Barry.
MR. BURPLE	Mr. W. Bellamy.	Mr. W. Robertson.
HENRY SCHAEL	Mr. A. F. Blake.	Mr. L. H. Everitt.
CHARLEY	Mr. I. Duncan.	Mr. Chapman.
JONES	Mr. J. Bilby.	Mr. S. Bradshaw.
MRS. BURPLE	Mrs. Axtel.	Mrs. Bradshaw.
CATHERINE	Miss F. Denham.	Miss A Wilks.

Costume.

HANS.—As a Turner. Linen coat and pants—red neckerchief—heavy red beard—Kossuth hat, &c.

MR. BURPLE.—Plain modern suit.

HENRY.—Ibid.

CHARLEY.—Ibid.

JONES —Black gown, &c.

MRS. BURPLE.—Old-fashioned short waist and skirt, of grey or brown.

CATHERINE—Plain, but very neat.

STAGE DIRECTIONS.

L. means *First Entrance, Left.* R. *First Entrance, Right.* S. E. L. *Second Entrance, Left.* S. E. R. *Second Entrance, Right.* U. E. L. *Upper Entrance, Left.* U. E. R. *Upper Entrance, Right.* C. *Centre.* L. C. *Left Centre.* R. C. *Right of Centre.* T. E. L. *Third Entrance, Left.* T. E. R. *Third Entrance, Right.* C. D. *Centre Door.* D. R. *Door Right.* D. L. *Door Left.* U. D. L. *Upper Door, Left* U. D. R. *Upper Door, Right.*

*** The reader is supposed to be on the Stage, facing the Audience

THE DUTCHMAN'S GHOST.

SCENE I.—*A Room in Burple's House. Bed, with curtains. Table, chairs, &c. Door,* R. 2. E.

Enter MR. *and* MRS. BURPLE, R.

Bur. I say not, my dear.

Mrs. B. And I say he is. So don't contradict me again, or I shall be compelled to resort to—— [*Shows key.*

Bur. I didn't mean it, my dear—I only wished to impress upon your mind that Hans is too far advanced in years for our daughter.

Mrs. B. How dare you question my judgment? Hans has a snug two-story frame, and something laid up beside. Hans carries on a large coffin manufactory.

Bur. So you look out for number one. Polished mahogany—silver plate—in case, my dear, anything should happen—you understand.

Mrs. B. Allow me to inform you, Mr. Burple, there's not so much good fortune in store for you, as the approaching of my latter end.

Bur. Mrs. B., I never expressed a wish or desire as regards your latter end. The contrary, my dear, I shall be rejoiced to see you live—all your life!

Mrs. B. I shall, my stupid, if only to oppose you in your absurdities. Were I to die to-day, the prospect is that to-morrow my precious remains would be disgraced by the absence of mahogany, and not so much as a daub of brick dust by way of ornament.

Bur. There you are wrong, my dear; for not long since, I ordered one of the most beautiful carriages I could find.

Mrs. B. Carriages, Mr, Burple!

Bur. Properly speaking, carriage—vulgar, coffin.

Mrs. B. For me?

Bur. Yes, my dear. Rosewood, with a most beautiful and costly plate, fifteen Spanish dollars worked up according to order, with your name in full, sufficient space for age, time of the happy event, &c. &c.

Mrs. B. You hard-hearted old wretch! you—you dilapidated specimen of villainy. A coffin for me! happy event! You shall lament this over a crust of bread and a glass of water in your favorite room.

Bur. My dear, allow me to——

Mrs. B. Not a word! You have confessed your guilt, and shal. suffer the penalty. So go!

Bur. Go! where?

Mrs. B. There! [*Pointing to door*, R. 2 E.] Are you going?

Bur Yes, my dear——

Mrs B. Go! [*Shoves him in and locks door.*

Bur [*Within.*] My dear, there's a window in this room fifty feet ground

Mrs. B. Then jump out of it!

Bur. I prefer the bread and water.

Mrs. B. I'm mistress, master, judge, and jury here. What I say's law—woman's rights triumphant! Not marry Hans!. We shall see Here comes Catherine. I'll try persuasion—if that won't do, I know what will.

Enter CATHERINE, L. H.

Catherine, my dear, come here.

Cath. [*Aside.*] How changed—"my dear." Mother.

Mrs. B. Catherine, do you love your mother?

Cath. Love *you*, mother! Yes, when you do not scold me.

Mrs. B. Scold you, child! you know 'tis not my nature. Care of my family has at times excited me to harsh words, perhaps to scold *you*, but then, my dear, 'twas always for your good.

Cath. Yes, mother; but you should know the disposition of your child—you would find that loving words have far more, and better effect, than all the harsh commands you can use.

Mrs. B. [*Aside.*] We shall see. Listen to me, Catherine. You are now of that age when young ladies look about them for a worthy object, on whom they may place their affections; you, I suppose, are not unlike others, so I imagine you have done the same already.

Cath No, mother, no.

Mrs. B. No! no favorite little beaux?

Cath. None.

Mrs. B. That's fortunate. Catherine, let me advise you. Beware of those pretty fellows, for almost invariably these pretty fellows, in their handsome liveries, (not paid for, some,) can scarcely support themselves, let alone a wife and half-a-dozen squalling brats. When I married your father, he was pretty well to do, and he, (knowing me to be a kind, virtuous, sincere, and economical girl,) could not do better than marry.

Cath. Yes, mother, you were fortunate to obtain so good a husband.

Mrs. B. The reverse, my dear. As regards yourself, I think that I have made a very good choice; to be sure he is not very young, nor very good-looking; he has money—money and age can pass where youth, beauty and poverty dare not enter. A widower, with money - only one child—company, my dear, company.

Cath. And this husband you've selected for me?

Mrs. B. I have, my dear. Now do I not love you?

Cath. Mother, I have not loved yet.

Mrs. B. Romantic nonsense! You will, my dear, when you shall hear the music of his coin.

Cath. A person perhaps I have never seen.

Mrs. B. Oh, yes, my dear; a friend of the family.

Cath. Who, pray, mother, is it?

Mrs. B. Hans Barth.

Cath. Mother!

Mrs. B. Catherine!

Cath. He's old enough to be my father.

Mrs. B. He has money, my dear.

Cath. Foolish, ignorant, miserly——

Mrs. B. He has money, my dear.

Cath. I never did, nor never can *like* him.

Mrs. B. You can love—his money. Catherine, will you marry Hans, provided he can make himself agreeable?

Cath. That he can never do, nor will I marry him.

Mrs. B. Not for your dear, kind old mother?

Cath. Not without my heart's consent.

Mrs. B. You impudent, thoughtless little hussy. Your heart's consent! what's that, compared to a mother's? Undutiful child! you will break you poor mother's heart!

Cath. Mother!

Mrs. B. Silence—not a word! hush—sh! He'll be here directly; receive him with respect; love—his money; or I'll lock you up, I'll tear—— [*Going*, L., *meets* HANS.

Enter HANS, L. H.

Ah, Mr. Hans! we were expecting you.

Hans. Vie cates!

Mrs. B. Sim lict goot, Mr. Hans.

Hans. Miss Catherine, spraken se Tuych? [*Crosses to* CATHERINE. Spraken se Tuych?

Cath. [*Very loud.*] Nein!

Hans. [*Retreating to corner.*] Nein! tat means no. Un tat means yaw, tis is te first dime I know nein means yaw. Miss Catherine, you spraken se burty goot tuych; goot, lout!

Mrs. B. Oh, yes; Catherine's German is very good. You are aware that she is of German descent?

Hans. Yaw, I suppose she is decent—I ton't know.

Mrs. B. You do not understand. Though born——

Hans. Yaw, I suppose she was born—I ton't know.

Mrs. B. Though born in this country——

Hans. I ton't know—I vas not tere, but I suppose it vas all right.

Mrs. B. Mr. Hans, I mean——

Hans. Tat what everypody say you are—tam mean old woman!

Mrs. B. Do you think so, Mr. Hans?

Hans. I dinks what everybody dinks.

Mrs. B. Can you speak of me so slight?

Hans. I don't know—I suppose it is all right.

Mrs. B. It is not right, Mr. Hans. I am not mean, and to prove it, I've considered the wish you expressed to me the other day, and assure you that you have my consent. What do you say now?

Hans. I suppose it is all right.

Mrs. B. You may depend upon it. Catherine, my dear, here's ninety dollars for the needful. [*Gives purse.*] Mr. Hans, suppose you walk out with Catherine, and display your taste in the selection of the finery. Be careful, my son; Catherine loves you very dearly, so do not trifle with her litttle heart. [*Exit* MRS. BURPLE, L. H.

Hans. I suppose it is all right.

Cath. [*Aside.*] What shall I do? If I humor him in his foolish hopes, something *may* occur to relieve my oppressed heart. It shall be so. [*Aloud.*] Mr. Hans, they have left us all alone.

Hans. Yaw! I suppose it is all right. Miss Catherine, you are peautiful gal—so peautiful pehint as pefore!

Cath. As beautiful, Mr. Hans, as the late Mrs. Barth?

Hans. Oh, ho—she is tiet. She tie teat von tay mit herself—tat is a fact. I suppose it vas all right.

Cath. The remembrance causes pain.

Hans. Nein! she say tere vas nix pain. She say tat she vas glat she tie teat. She say it vas all right, un I suppose it vas all right, do.

Cath. You were deeply affected!

Hans. Yaw! on my nose mit te proom-stick. She give me te duyvel sometimes mit tat fellow. Now she is teat, I ton't got affected mit te proomstick some more. Now it is all right.

Cath. You now find that a wife is a positive necessary?

Hans. Yaw! I shall be teat mit myself if I ton't got some more frow—tat is a fact. Tat nunder von vas tie tead, vas she duyvel—you are peautiful angel; I love you all over, from te top fon your heat do tat shoes fon your feet. You have some leetle foots—tat nunder frow, vas has gone teat, has some tam pig foots, un every night she kicks me out fon te floor on top te ped.

Cath. Is it possible?

Hans. Yaw! ten, by tam, she say it is all right.

Cath. So, Mr. Hans, you find that a loving heart is preferable to physical or pugilistic accomplishments?

Hans. Yaw, Miss Catherine. I have tat love heart von top my waiscoat jacket. I dels you, when I vas leetle poy, no pigger as tas, te vomans say tat myself vas leetle Tuych Cupit; I vas so peautiful poy tat un Tuych country tere vas von grant fair tere, for peautiful fat Cupit papies, un my moter have got fon tat president fon tat fair—peautiful leater medal for her peautiful fat Cupit papy. Tat vas myself; tat is why you have some love for me. Your moter say you love me very much, un I love you very much, do. Vas peautiful hant, Miss Catherine! [*Kisses her hand. For a moment looks her full in the face, and clasps her in his arms—instantly releases her.*] Mine Got un Himel! tas is goot!

Cath. Mr. Hans, if you dare repeat your rudeness, I shall call for help.

Hans. Miss Catherine, I suppose it vas all right.

Cath. No, sir; not right to insult a lady.

Hans. Miss Catherine, I never consult you in my life. [*Aside.*] How I should like to kiss tat peautiful lips! [*Aloud.*] Miss Catherine, when you are my leetle frow, you shall have peautiful pran new second-hant silk tress, mate mit satin; un when you tie teat, you shall have tat splenit coffins mit silver outsites, vas I make for a fellow tat tie teat—he ton't come un got it yet. You use see, un ten you vill say it is all right.

Cath. You certainly are very considerate, Mr. Hans. You perfectly agree with Mr. Toodles.

Hans. Mr. Doodles! who is tat Mr. Doodles? I dell you I ton't care for Mr. Doodles! If Mr. Doodles consult you, I will preak Mr. Doodles' eye. You ton't love tat Doodles?

Cath. No! Mr. Hans——

Hans. Yaw; you love Mr. Hans—tat is myself. Mr. Doodles! tam tat Doodles!

Cath. No, no! you mistake—you do not understand, as the man says in the play. Mr. Toodles, in speaking of coffins, remarks how handy it is to have them in the house.

Hans. Yaw! ha! ha! ha! tat is a fact. Miss Catherine, give me some leetle kiss, un ten I forgive you mit a nunder von.

Cath. No, no, no!

Hans. But I say yaw, yaw, yaw!

[CATHERINE *retreats*, HANS *following.*

Cath. Help! help! Murder! [HANS *kisses her.*] Help!

Bur. [*Within.*] Hallo there! Help! Murder!

[BURPLE *bursts open door.* HANS, *making for door to escape, encounters* BURPLE—*making for door*, L., *encounters* MRS. BURPLE. CATHERINE *faints in chair.* BURPLE *falls*, R. MRS. BURPLE, L.—HANS, C.

Hans. I don't know—I suppose it is all right!!!

SCENE II.—*A Street.*

Enter HENRY, L.

Henry. Wo ho, Tim! See if you can stand still till I settle with the old man. A pretty heavy load and a devlish good pull you've made of it for a last one. [*Going*, R.

Enter CHARLEY, R.

Char. Hallo, Hen.! driving so late? I thought you were done all that, and about to embark into something more extensive, more respectable.

Henry. Charley, ar'n't it respectable to be an honest, hard-working man? Look at these—[*showing hands*]—they speak for themselves It's respectable to carry a pair like that, for any one could swear you don't steal.

Char. You do not understand me. I do not pretend to say that honest labor is not respectable. There are trades and professions that are looked upon as better, though they may not be so profitable as driving.

Henry. Driving! better professions! Ask my old dad—he'll tell you that when he was of my age, driving as you see me, without an old man to put dimes in his pocket and good clothes on his back, nobody cared for him; he saved money, bought a cart, then a dozen; a tract of land, worked it to advantage. Now he has lots of rocks, everybody knows my old dad; they want to make a Congressman of him. Dad's not such a fool—he has plenty, and don't care for anybody.

Char. I say, Hen., look there! a runaway—that girl—quick, for heaven's sake!

Henry. Have an eye on my horse.

[*Exit* HENRY, L. H. *Loud crash*, L. H.

Char. Go it, Hen. That's it—all right—now you have her! [*Crash.*

Enter HENRY, *supporting* CATHERINE.

Henry. Charley, some water! [*Exit* CHARLEY, R. H.] She's only frightened—the horses merely grazed her.

Enter CHARLEY, *with water*—HENRY *places it to* CATHERINE'S *lips.*

Cath. [*Reviving.*] No—the—I am not hurt. Thank you, sir—oh, thank you. You have saved my life.

Enter HANS, L. H.

Hans. [*Aside.*] I suppose it is all right now.

Henry. No thanks, miss, owe you me. I am only too happy to know that I have rescued you, and taught the coward his duty—the protection of his charge. [*To* HANS.

Hans. [*To* HENRY.] Well, I suppose it is all right!

Char. [*Crossing to* HANS.] I say; you're a shang!

Hans. Yaw! Vas is tas?

Char. You crow when you are out of danger. You're a Shanghai!

Hans. [*Aside.*] He says I am some hieshang. [*Aloud.*] you are a tam—funny fellow.

Char. Oh! I thought you hadn't spunk to say anything else.

Hans. Spunk! who is Spunk? I ton't got some what you gall Spunk. Spunk is 'frait fon a Tuychman—tat is what Spunk.

Char. Ha! ha! I respect you for speaking tho truth for the first time in your life. There! [CHARLEY *offers hand*—HANS *is about tc take it*—*he snatches it away, which causes* HANS *to turn into corner.* L.

Hans. My Got un Himel! tat is a funny fellow! I suppose it is all right.

Char. Yes, all right. Ha! ha! ha!

Henry. [*Coming down with* CATHERINE.] So, then, Miss Burple, I shall see you again?

Cath. I shall always be happy to receive you.

Hans. Yaw! yaw! I suppose it is all right.

Henry. I was not speaking to you, sir. For such a prize, I'd risk my life a dozen times—eh, Charley? or you—why did *you* not assist her?

Hans. Nein! She is not my sister, but by un by she will pe my little frow—wife.

Henry. Wife!

Cath. [*Aside to* HENRY.] No, sir, no. [*Going.*

Henry. Stay, Miss Burple; may I not have the pleasure of conducting you to your home?

Cath. Certainly, sir; for then my parents will add their blessing to mine for the preserver of their child. [*Taking* HENRY'S *arm.*

Henry. I don't want to be troubled with intruders. Charley, please have an eye on my horse, and take care of the Dutchman. This way, miss. [*Exit, with* CATHERINE, R. H. 1 E. HANS *attempts to follow*—CHARLEY *detains him.*

Char. Don't be in a hurry, old fellow.

Hans. I have bustiness. I ton't care. I dell you, if my frow vas is gone teat, hear you gall her husband—tat is myself—old fellow, she woult preak tat proom-stick mit your heat.

[*Going*—CHARLEY *stops him.*

Char. She was some, then, on a fight, old fellow.

Hans. Don't you gall me tat, ton't you!

Char. Why, old fellow'?

Hans. You use spraken se tat again!

Char. To oblige you, certainly, old fellow.

Hans. I suppose it is all right. Now I shall go. By un py, day after yesterday, py tam, you will see. [*Going*, R., CHARLEY *turns him round to corner*, L.] Py tam, I will fight you!

Char. Oh, very well!

Hans. [*Taking off coat, &c.*] Very well—you ton't know—you will see—what—— I suppose it is all right. How I will plow your nose off—now—now, by tam—[*coming boldly up to* CHARLEY]—well?

Char. Well?

Hans. I suppose—— [CHARLEY *suddenly trips him, and runs off, laughing.*] Come back un fight mit me. Cowart! I suppose it is all right. [*Endeavors to rise.*] No, py tam, 'tis not all right. I know vas I vill to—I will gone away un get te bost office to but himself on dop of te dooms. It is all right. Nein! My Got un Himel! I have te gunstumption in my stomejack! [*Exit* HANS, L.

SCENE III.—*Same as Scene 1.*

Enter MR. *and* MRS. BURPLE, R. H.

Mrs. B. At last you have come to your proper senses, and conclude that Hans is the most fitting person on whom to bestow our daughter.

Bur. Yes, my dear, I have thought over it seriously, and am precisely of your way of thinking.

Mrs. B. Let a young girl marry a man who has nothing but good looks and sweet speech to recommend him, ten to one, in less than a year she'll be back on her parents, or compelled to look out for herself. [*Knock*, L. D.] Come in.

Enter CATHERINE *and* HENRY.

Catherine, where's Hans?

Cath. I know not, mother; he deserted me when I was in danger; his duty devolved on this young man, who saved my life at hazard of his own.

Mr. and Mrs. B. Saved your life!

Cath. Yes. Suffice it to say, that while crossing our most busy thoroughfare, a pair of horses, with fright, broke from a carriage, and would have trampled me to death, when this young man, perceiving my dangerous situation, with one hand grasped the reins, and with the other raised me from beneath the horses' feet. Receive him as the preserver of your child; my life I owe to him. Mr. Henry Schael—my father, my mother.

Mrs. B. Pshaw! Hans could have done the same.

Henry. Yes, if he'd the courage, which is a stranger to the one who was her companion.

Bur. Young man, we thank you. [*To* CATHERINE.] Where's your future husband—where's Hans?

Hans. [*Looking on at* L. 1 E.] Tat is myself! Her I vas—it is all right.

Bur. Mr. Hans, it seems you were very careful of your safety to allow this young man the glory of rescuing Catherine, when you might have done it just as well as he.

Hans. Yaw! It vas myself! I shump von top tat horse's back, tat was pehint, like tat, un ten I dake his dail, tat vas pehint, do, like tat, un ten he ton't go some more before, but shump up pehint like tat, un ten——

Mrs. B. What then?

Hans. I shump town and rund avay.

Mrs. B. Mr. Hans, you **will** thank the young man for his assistance.

Hans. Yaw! I vill to tat. Young man, you are goot young man—you are prave young man, as never vas. I tank you burty goot, un I vill make you present—of a sixpence, for lager pier. Tere.

Henry. And there! [*Knocking it out of his hand.*

Hans. I don't know—I suppose it is all right!

[*Picking it up and putting it in his pocket.*

Henry Is this your gratitude—this my return for the preservation of your child? I am rewarded. She, at least, is grateful. She loves me. I'll tell you something else. I love her.

Hans. You love my frow tat is to pe!

Henry. I love this lady—your wife that's not to be.

Hans. You love her! You say tat?

Henry. Yes. [*Walking closely up to* HANS.] Don't you like it?

Hans. [*Moving off.*] Yaw! yaw! I ton't know—I suppose it is all right.

Mrs. B. I'll make it right. Young man, we thank you for your assistance to our daughter; trusting that is all-sufficient, we bid you good evening.

Hans. Goot bye, young man—it is all right now!

Mrs. B. You, miss, shall become Mrs. Barth, or in this room shall you eat, drink, and sleep till you willingly consent to marry Hans!

[*Going up with* BURPLE.

Hans. Now it is all right. Young man. tere is some door!

[*Going up to* MRS. B.

Henry. [*Aside.*] This room! Ah! a window! Catherine, will you be mine?

Cath. [*Aside.*] I will!

Henry. [*Aside to* CATHERINE.] From that window, to-night, I can rescue you without danger. [*Aloud.*] Farewell, miss. Remember that in me you have a friend that will not desert you when you are in danger. For you, [*to* MR. *and* MRS. B.,] I freely forgive you, and trust that time may teach you to love, not despise, the worthy.

[*Exit* HENRY, L. H.

Mrs. B. So, Miss Romance, you'll be off with this young whipper-snapper, because he happens to help you out of the gutter; and in spite of all your kind old mother's advice, you'll be going to the d——but you shan't—you shall marry Hans! Come along, Mr. Burple.

Bur. Yes, my dear. And in case of an attempt at a rescue, I'll load my old blunderbuss with a good dose of powder and peas.

Mrs. B. [*Locking door.*] I think Miss, you'll alter your opinion before morning. Hans, my son, there's your wife, and when you're sleepy, there's a bed. [*Exit* MR. *and* MRS. BURPLE, R. H.

Hans. Miss Catherine, I suppose it is all right. Tat door is locked, un tat door is locked, un tere is some ped. I will go sloughpen mit myself. I suppose—— [*Going towards bed.*

Cath. Oh, Mr. Hans! don't—don't go near that bed!

Hans. My Got un Himel! why I ton't go tere?

Cath. Are you ignorant of the fearful deed that was perpetrated here?

Hans. Nein! Your fater dells me kills 'bout five huntred rats tere.

Cath. He has never informed you of that inhuman murder?

Hans. My Got un Himel! nein.

Cath Hush! [CATHERINE *takes chair—pantomimes for* HANS *to do the same.* HANS *goes up.* CATHERINE *lets chair fall.*

Hans. Vas is tas? I dink it vas te duyvel!

Cath. You are not frightened?

Hans. Nein! I ton't got frait; I am a Tuychman. It is all right.

[*Brings down chair.*

Cath. You see yonder bed?

Hans. Yaw.

Cath. No human being has dared to rest there since the death of my great grandfather. For the last hundred years, every morning, that bed has been regularly made, and as regularly occnpied at night, though no one was ever seen to enter this room after dark.

Hans. Berhaps it vas te duyvel. He stays out so late tat when he goes home, he vas locked out, un ten he sloughpen tere, to save twelve un a half cent for lozenges.

Cath. No, it is the spirit of the dead.

Hans [*Aside, drinking.*] I shall go teat if I ton't got some spirit.

Cath. No one has had courage to demand his secret. You will, Mr. Hans.

Hans. No, by tam! I tank you. Excuse me, Miss Catherine's great grandfather's spirit—'tis none of my bustiness. I suppose it is all right.

Cath. On the night of the 20th of August, 1756, my great grandfather retired to rest in that bed. About midnight, the family were roused from their slumber by the cries of "Murder!" proceeding from this apartment. My grandfather rushed in just in time to receive the dying breath of his father, which whispered "Murdered." Since that time, on every succeeding night of that date, the same horrible cries are heard to issue from this room, which are calculated to strike terror to the bravest heart.

Hans. [*Aside.*] My Got un Himel! I wish I vas home.

Cath. To-night is the 20th; so we shall have a chance of observing what passes, should the spirit appear.

HENRY *and* CHARLEY *enter at window, observed by* CATHERINE, *and conceal themselves behind bed.*

You have, I'm sure, sufficient courage.

Hans. Yaw; I have some Tuych courage. You have some goot schnapps? [*Drinking.*

Cath. No, my Hans, I prefer a little repose. I shall rest in this chair.

Hans. Very well, I ton't care. Hans, my poy, you are prave Tuychman; you ton't got frait fon spirits. Tere is some courage left. [*Drinks.*] Miss Catherine, you vill kiss me goot pye, pecause if te duyvel come here, I am a gone Tuychman. My tear, peautiful——

[*About to kiss her.*

Henry. [*Very loud, from bed.*] Forbear!

Hans. My Got un Himel! vas is tas?

Cath. What, Mr. Hans?

Hans. Don you hear tat?

Cath. No.

Hans. I dink it vas te duyvel.

Cath. Pshaw!

Hans. I vas going to kiss your peautiful lips, un te duyvel say, "Borfare, you tam Tuychman!"

Cath. Then I am protected by my great grandfather's spirit!

Hans. Is te duyvel your great grandfather? My Got un Himel!

Henry. Hans Barth!

Hans. Tat is myself!

Henry. Hans Barth!

Hans. Tat is te duyvel!

Henry. Hans Barth!

Hans. I do not furstay English, Mr. Miss Catherine's great grandfather's spirit

Henry. If you dare profane with a touch that sacred form of innocence, reserved for holier love, death be thy portion!!!

Hans. Don't been afrait, Miss Catherine's great grandfather's spirit; I ton't touch tat peautiful innocence. Miss Catherine. She's sloughpen! What shall I do if——

[HENRY *strikes bed*—CHARLEY *dances pillow on broom-stick*—HANS *endeavors to call for help, falls on his knees.* HENRY *assists* CATHERINE *out of window—when fairly out,* CHARLEY *comes down with terrible noise, throws sheet over* HANS, *fires pistol, and hastily exits through window.* MR. *and* MRS. BURPLE *come on,* R. H.—*light goes out*—BURPLE *goes towards window, turns, perceives* HANS, *fires gun*—HANS *falls.* SERVANT *brings on light.* HANS *throws off sheet.*

Omnes. Hans Barth!

Hans. I don't know—I suppose it is all right!!!

SCENE IV.—*A Street.*

Enter HANS, R. H.

Hans. By dinks now it is all right. I know it *vas* Miss Catherine's great grandfather's ghost. I dink tat dime I vas gone Tuycha. I dinks I dink I vas plown up mit little pieces, into te mittle of tay pefore yesterday. Hans, my poy, you ton't got frait—nein! By tam, if te duyvel vas tere, Hans would say——My Got un Himel! vas is tas? [*Conceals himself,* R. H.

Enter CHARLEY, CATHERINE, *and* HENRY, L.

Henry. This way! this way! In a few moments, you will be beyond the reach of those you fear. My father's house shall shelter you from all danger.

Char. Come, then, for they are at our heels. This way, Miss; it's only above here. Mr. Schael's two doors from the corner of the next street, which is seventh.

Henry. Yes, lose not a moment.

Cath. Henry, will you protect me?

Henry. With my life! Come, this way! [*Exeunt,* R. H.

Hans. [*Coming down.*] Ah ha! py tam, I have got you now. *Now it is all right!* Tat fellow has some bustiness mit Miss Catherine's great grandfather's ghost.

Enter MR. *and* MRS. BURPLE, L. H.

Ah ha! it is all right now! I have tat fellow vas steal avay Miss Catherine. I see her, do, mit my two eyes. Tat fellow say he vill dake her mit his fater, Mr. Schael, who vas live use above tere, dwo doors fon tat corner of tat next street, vat is sevent.

Bur. Come then, and rescue her at once.

Mrs. B. No, that will never do. We must trick them. I have a plan that shall not only restore her, but unite her to the man of our choice. Mr. Burple, do you discover where she is; then, with tears in your eyes, inform her that her poor mother now lies cold and lifeless in the home she has disgraced. In the meantime, I shall provide a proper person to perform the marriage ceremony, which she cannot escape if I once lay my hands upon her.

Hans. Yaw! tat is goot! You go home un tie teat, un ten it vill be all right.

Bur. A good trap! We are certain of success!

Hans. Yaw! Dake care you ton't got you foot in it; pecause if you do, be tam if it will pe all right.

[*Exit* BURPLE *and* HANS, R.—MRS. B., L.

SCENE V.—*Chamber, same as before.*

Enter MRS. BURPLE *and* JONES, R. H.

Mrs B. Mr. Jones, retire to that room, and be prepared for the signal. I expect them every moment. [*Knock*, L.] Come in.

Enter HANS, L.

Hans. It is all right. So soon as te old man say tat you have gone teat, Miss Catherine laugh like te duyvel.

Mrs. B. Laugh!

Hans. Yaw! mit—vas you gall tat fellow?—hystericals. Py tam, she laugh, un ten she tance mit her feet, dill she cry mit her eyes.

Mrs. B. And is she coming?

Hans. Yaw! ha! ha! ha! she come to see her poor teat moter. We vill have some fun, un ten I vill have some frow—ten, by *tam*, it vill be all right.

Mrs. B. Hans, be prepared. The bed for me. [*Going to bed.*

Hans. My Got un Himel! ton't go tere! Miss Catherine's great grandfather's ghost——[*Knock at door*, L.] Come in.

Enter BURPLE *and* CATHERINE, L. H.

Cath. Where is my poor, dear, dead mother?

Mrs. B. [*Sitting up.*] Catherine, my dear!

Cath. My mother alive!

Hans. Yaw, by tam, un kicking.

[MRS. B. *brings* CATHERINE *down*, C. HENRY *and* CHARLEY, *with gun, enter at window, and conceal themselves behind bed.*

Ah ha! we have got you now!

Char. [*Peeping from curtain.*] And we'll have you directly.

Bur. Catherine, the only alternative is to marry Hans, your mother's choice. That alone will reconcile everything.

Char [*Aside.*] I'd like to reconcile you. [*Pointing gun.*

Hans. Yaw, and make it all right.

Char. [*Aside.*] This fellow would like to make you all right.

[CATHERINE *discovers* CHARLEY, *&c.*

Mrs. B. There is but one way, and it is this. [*Goes to door*, R.] This way, Mr. Jones!

Enter JONES.

We are prepared.

Char. [*Aside.*] So are we.

Hans. Yaw! we are prepared.

Cath. And so am I. [*Part aside to* HENRY.

Hans. Ten, Mr. Shones, make it all right. Miss Catherinee—— [*About to take her hand.*

Henry. [*From bed.*] Forbear!

[HANS *drops* CATHERINE'S *hand, and falls on his knees.*

Hans. My Got un Himel! it is Miss Catherine's great grandfather's spirit!

Cath. Tremble all, for I am protected!

Henry. Hans Barth!

Hans. My Got un Himel! vas vils too haben, Miss Catherine's great grandfather's ghost?

Henry. Remember!—Dare but unite your fate with that of purity, innocence and love—dare profane with a look, that sacred form, and fire shall consume your false and guilty heart! Beware!!!

Hans. My Got un Himel! Miss Catherine's great grandfather's ghost, you will forgive me. I am a tam Tuych villain! un I vill not brofane tat peautiful innocence mit burty love. It vas not myself—it vas tat old beoples!

Mrs. and Mrs. B. No! no! no!

Henry. Peace! Are you willing she should bestow her hand where she has already given her heart?

Omnes. { We are!
Yaw! yaw!

Henry. [*Coming down.*] Thon behold her future husband!

Mrs. B. Ah! a trick! Mr. Jones, proceed! Hans, take Catherine's hand!

Hans. Yaw! Un ten, Miss Catherine's great grandfather's ghost, [*to* HENRY,] it vill pe all right. [*About to take* CATHERINE'S *hand.*

Char. [*Pointing gun from bed.*] Drop that! or look out for the fire!

Hans. My Got un Himel! vas is tas? It is te duyvel, or some more of Miss Catherine's great grandfather's ghosts.

Char. [*Jumping out of bed.*] Hen., take your wife that is to be. Have you any objections, or you, or you? I'm sure you have none. [*To* CATHERINE.] Have you? [*To* HANS.

Hans. Nein, Mr. Duyvel-Skin! I have nix rejections.

Char. [*To* MR. *and* MRS. B.] You may as well give your consent. He's a good boy, and will make Catherine a *good husband.* He saved her life, and has fairly won her.

Henry. Forget and forgive. I assure you that you will never regret the moment you gave your willing consent for Catherine to marry an honest man.

Mrs. B. There, take her! she is yours! Be happy!

Henry. And you, sir?

Mrs. B. I speak for myself and him, too.

Henry. What say you? [*To* HANS.

Hans. Mr. Duyvel-Skin, you are a funny poy, un Miss Catherine's great grandfather's ghost, you have my constant. *New it is all right!*

Char. All are happy!
Henry. And all content!
Cath. There are others. Ask them [*to audience*] their consent?
Mrs. B. Not I. My dear, say something, do.
Bur. No, madam; I'll leave that for you.
You've had the say, me the fag;
'Tis not, my business, madam,
To speak the tag.
Henry Hans, here's a chance for you.
Hans. Vas, must I spraken some spoken, do?
Ladies and gentlemen:—A Dutchman mit his tricks
Have lose his frow, un get exactly nix.
For *you* I suffer all do-night;
Say you are bleased; if so,

ALL RIGHT!

THE END.

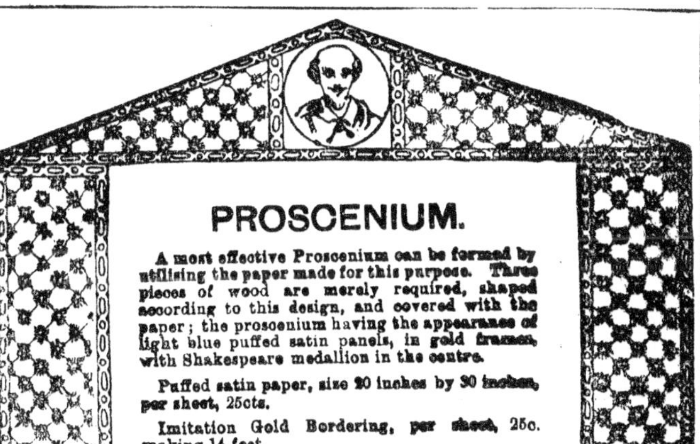

PROSCENIUM.

A most effective Proscenium can be formed by utilising the paper made for this purpose. Three pieces of wood are merely required, shaped according to this design, and covered with the paper; the proscenium having the appearance of light blue puffed satin panels, in gold frames, with Shakespeare medallion in the centre.

Puffed satin paper, size 20 inches by 30 inches, per sheet, 25cts.

Imitation Gold Bordering, per sheet, 25c. making 14 feet.

Shakespearian Medallion, 18 inches in diameter, 50cts.

DOORS.—These comprise three sheets of paper each, and can be had either for drawing-room or cottage purposes. Size, 7 feet by 8 feet. Price, complete, $1.25 each.

WINDOW.—This is a parlour window formed with two sheets of paper, and could be made practicable to slide up and down. The introduction of curtains each side would make it very effective. Size, 3 feet by 4½ feet. Price, $1.00, complete.

FIREPLACE.—This is also made with two sheets of paper. The fire is lighted, but should this not be required a fire-paper can be hung over it. It will be found most useful in many farces wherein a character has to climb up a chimney, and many plays where a fireplace is indispensable. By purchasing a door, window, and fireplace an ordinary room scene could easily be constructed with the addition of some wall-paper. Size 3 ft. by 4½ ft. Price, complete, $1.25.

MAKE-UP BOX

Tin Case, $5.00. Cloth Board, $4.00.

Contains everything necessary for making up the face, viz.:—Rouge, Pearl Powder, Whiting, Mongolian, Ruddy Rouge, Powdered Antimony, Joining Paste, Violet Powder, Box and Puff; Chrome, Blue, Burnt Cork, Pencils for the Eyelids, Spirit Gum, Indian Ink, Burnt Umber, Camel Hair Brushes, Hares' Foot, Wool, Crape Hair, Cold Cream, Paint Saucer, Miniature Puffs, Scissors and Looking Glass. Each article is of the best quality. Packed neatly in a Strong Cloth-covered Box, $4; Elegant Tin Case, $5. We can strongly recommend the Tin cases. They are very durable, and any article can be used without disturbing another, a great advantage in making-up.

The above articles to be had separately. See preceding pages.

FRENCH'S ACTING EDITIONS,

PRICE, 15cts. EACH.

NEW PLAYS.

Bitter Reckoning
Eileen Oge
Bathing
An Old Score
My Sister from India
Maria Martin
Among the Relics
Nabob for an Hour
An Old Man
Village Nightingale
Our Nelly
Partners for Life
Chopstick and Spikins
Chiselling
Birds in their Little Nests
Pretty Predicament
Seven Sins
Insured at Lloyd's
Hand and Glove
Keep Your Eye on Her
Jessamy's Courtship
False Alarm
Up in the World
Parted
One in Hand, &c.
Little Sunshine
Who'll Lend me a Wife
Extremes Meet
Golden Plough
Sweethearts
Velvet and Rags
Cut for Partner
Love's Alarm
An Appeal to the Feelings
Tale of a Comet
Under False Colors
Heroes
Philanthropy
Little Vixens
Telephone
Too Late to Save
Just My Luck
Grateful Father
Happy Medium
Sole Survivor
Neck or Nothing
Poppleton's Predicaments
Auld Acquaintance
Weeds
White Pilgrim
Dentist's Clerk
Lancers
Lucille
Randall's Thumb
Wicked World
Two Orphans
'Twixt Axe and Crown
Wonderful Woman
Curious Case
Forty Winks
Lady Clancarty
Never Too Late to Mend
Lily of France
Led Astray, 25 cts.
Henry V., new version
Unequal Match
May, or Dolly's Delusion
As Like as Two Peas
Court Cards
Happy Land
Allatoona
Enoch Arden
Weak Woman
How She Loves Him
Our Society
Mother-in-Law
Snowed In
Terrible Tinker
My Uncle's Will
Our Friends
Queen of Hearts
Lady of Lyons Married and Settled
Bitter Cold
Peacock's Holiday
Daisy Farm
Wrinkles
Lancashire Lass
On an Island
Q. E. D.
Withered Leaves
Ruth's Romance
Old Sailor
Pampered Menials
Noblesse Oblige
Lad from the Country
Not False but Fickle
Infatuation
Davenport Bros. & Co.
Freezing a Mother-in-Law
That Dreadful Doctor
Plot for Plot
Our Relatives
Engaged
My Awful Dad
On Bail
Tom Cobb
Bow Bells
Married for Money
Funnibone's Fix
Patter versus Clatter
For her Child's Sake
Married in Haste
Our Boys
Which
My Father's Will
Daniel Rochat
Caste
School
Home
David Garrick
Ours
Social Glass
Daniel Druce
Pinafore
Old Soldier
My Daughter's Début
Word of Honor
Sold Again
Guy Fawkes
Little Madcap
Handsome Jack
Scarlet Dick
Wedding March
My Wife's Father's Sister
His Novice
Much too Clever
Hamlet Improved

ARTICLES, NEEDED BY AMATEURS,

Such as Tableaux Lights, Magnesium Tableaux Lights, Prepared Burnt Cork, Grease, Paints, Lightning for Private Theatricals.

Guide to Selecting Plays, Hints on Costume, Scenery to fit any Stage.

Jarley's Wax Works, Ethiopian Plays, Charades, Amateur's Guide, Guide to the Stage.

NEW CATALOGUE SENT FREE.

SAMUEL FRENCH & SON,

38 E. 14th Street, Union Square, N. Y.

www.ingramcontent.com/pod-product-compliance
Lightning Source LLC
LaVergne TN
LVHW020636110826
845149LV00004B/1225

* 9 7 8 1 4 1 8 1 9 0 8 9 7 *